KU-417-350

Say What You See

Eat

Rebecca Rissman

700041457378

Raintree is an imprint of Capstone Global Library Limited, a company incorporated in England and Wales having its registered office at 7 Pilgrim Street, London, EC4V 6LB – Registered company number: 6695582

www.raintreepublishers.co.uk
myorders@raintreepublishers.co.uk

Text © Capstone Global Library Limited 2013
First published in hardback in 2013
Paperback edition first published in 2014
The moral rights of the proprietor have been asserted.

All rights reserved. No part of this publication may be reproduced in any form or by any means (including photocopying or storing it in any medium by electronic means and whether or not transiently or incidentally to some other use of this publication) without the written permission of the copyright owner, except in accordance with the provisions of the Copyright, Designs and Patents Act 1988 or under the terms of a licence issued by the Copyright Licensing Agency, Saffron House, 6–10 Kirby Street, London EC1N 8TS (www.cla.co.uk). Applications for the copyright owner's written permission should be addressed to the publisher.

Edited by Rebecca Rissman, Daniel Nunn, and
  Catherine Veitch
Designed by Philippa Jenkins
Picture research by Ruth Blair
Production by Victoria Fitzgerald
Originated by Capstone Global Library
Printed and bound in China

ISBN 978 1 406 25141 8 (hardback)
16 15 14 13 12
10 9 8 7 6 5 4 3 2 1

ISBN 978 1 406 25146 3 (paperback)
18 17 16 15 14
10 9 8 7 6 5 4 3 2 1

British Library Cataloguing in Publication Data
Rissman, Rebecca.
Eat. -- (Say What You See!)
394.1'2-dc23
A full catalogue record for this book is available from the British Library.

Acknowledgements
We would like to thank the following for permission to reproduce photographs: Shutterstock pp. title page (© ravl), 4 (© Nattika), 5 (© Charlotte Lake, © Petr Malyshev, © Bratwustle), 6 (© Ieva Vincer), 7 (© Petro Feketa, © Analia Valeria Urani), 8 (© discpicture), 9 (© trevorb), 10 (© Gunnar Pippel, © Monkey Business Images), 12 (© 3445128471), 13 (© .shock, © corepics), 15 (© Africa Studio, © Jiri Hera), 16 (© JohanKalen), 17 (© Andrey Armyagov, © Firma V), 18 (© ssuaphotos), 19 (© T-3, © .shock, © oknoart), 20 (© Rob Marmion), 21 (© MikLav, © Gorilla), 22 (© Monkey Business Images); Superstock pp. 9 (© Flirt), 11 (© Blend Images), 13 (© Fancy Collection), 14 (© Corbis), 15 (© BlueMoon Stock).

Cover photograph of a girl taking a bite out of a watermelon reproduced with permission of iStockphoto (© Kim Gunkel).

Every effort has been made to contact copyright holders of material reproduced in this book. Any omissions will be rectified in subsequent printings if notice is given to the publisher.

Contents

Breakfast is cooking...
Say what you see!

frying

stirring

Pouring

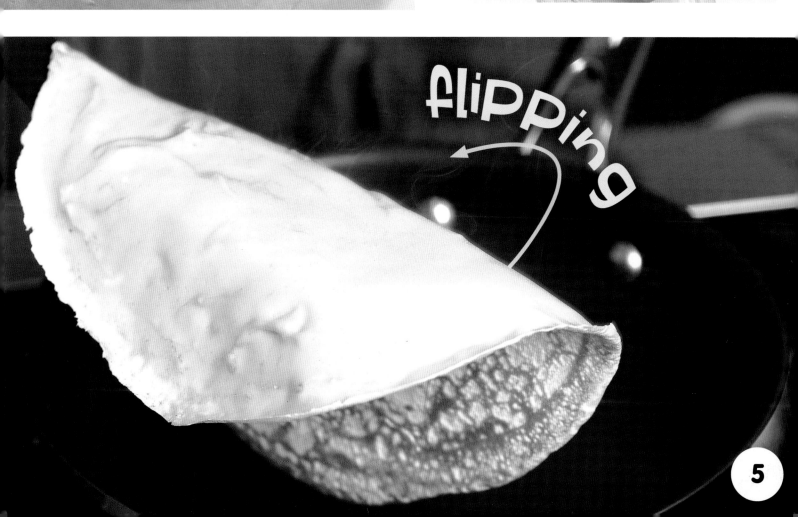

flipping

5

peeling

Baking

Whisking

Boiling

Scrambling

It's nearly time for lunch...
Say what you see!

Crunching

slurping slurping

Slicing

Grilling

Blending

Tossing

13

Scooping

Dipping

Spreading

Chopping

15

It's dinner time...
Say what you see!

Twisting

Chewing

Cutting

Roasting

Rising

Melting

Steaming

Eating gives us energy for...
growing!

Playing!

Thinking!

We eat to be healthy...
and because food tastes great!

Can you find these things in the book? Look back... and say what you see!

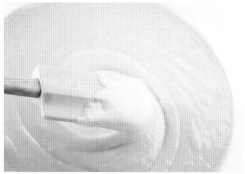

stirring

slicing

crunching

melting

Index